WHAT IS THE SUPREME COURT?

We the People:
U.S. Government at Work

Kevin Winn

Published in the United States of America by:

Cherry Lake Press
2395 South Huron Parkway, Suite 200, Ann Arbor, Michigan 48104
www.cherrylakepress.com

Reading Adviser: Beth Walker Gambro, MS, Ed., Reading Consultant, Yorkville, IL
Content Adviser: Mark Richards, Ph.D., Professor, Dept. of Political Science, Grand Valley State University, Allendale, MI

Photo Credits: cover: © Pablo Russo/Shutterstock; page 5: © Bob Korn/Shutterstock; page 6: © Everett Collection/Shutterstock; page 7: © TREKPix/Shutterstock; pages 8, 9 (top), 13 (bottom left, bottom right), 14, 15: Collection of the Supreme Court of the United States; page 9: Ralph Alswang/William J. Clinton Library/The National Archives (bottom); pages 11, 19: Library of Congress; page 12: © Art Lien; page 13: Chronicling America, Library of Congress (top); page 16: © fizkes/Shutterstock; page 20: © CW-Chill Out/ Shutterstock; page 21: © mentatdgt/Shutterstock

Cherry Lake Press is an imprint of Cherry Lake Publishing Group.

Library of Congress Cataloging-in-Publication Data

Names: Winn, Kevin P., author.
Title: What is the Supreme Court? / written by Kevin Winn.
Description: Ann Arbor, Michigan : Cherry Lake Publishing, [2023] | Series: We the people : U. S. government at work | Audience: Grades 2-3
Summary: "Young readers will discover what the Supreme Court is and what it does and learn about the basic building blocks of the United States of America. They'll also learn about how they play a key role in American democracy. Series is aligned to 21st Century Skills curriculum standards. Engaging inquiry-based sidebars encourage students to Think, Create, Guess, and Ask Questions. Includes table of contents, glossary, index, author biography, and sidebars"– Provided by publisher.
Identifiers: LCCN 2022039947 | ISBN 9781668919408 (hardcover) | ISBN 9781668920428 (paperback) | ISBN 9781668923085 (pdf) | ISBN 9781668921753 (ebook)
Subjects: LCSH: United States. Supreme Court–Juvenile literature. | Courts of last resort–United States–Juvenile literature.
Classification: LCC KF8742 .W56 2023 | DDC 347.73/26–dc23/eng/20220930
LC record available at https://lccn.loc.gov/2022039947

Cherry Lake Press would like to acknowledge the work of the Partnership for 21st Century Learning, a Network of Battelle for Kids. Please visit http://www.battelleforkids.org/networks/p21 for more information.

Printed in the United States of America
Corporate Graphics

CONTENTS

HISTORY OF THE SUPREME COURT

The United States government has three branches. These are the executive, legislative, and judicial branches. The Supreme Court is part of the judicial branch. It is the highest court in the land. Its job is to decide if laws follow the Constitution. Working with the president and Congress, the Supreme Court helps keep the government running.

The Supreme Court Building is in Washington, D.C.

The Constitution didn't exist when the United States became an official country. Instead, it followed the Articles of Confederation. People realized there were problems with the Articles of Confederation. One issue was that there was no court system.

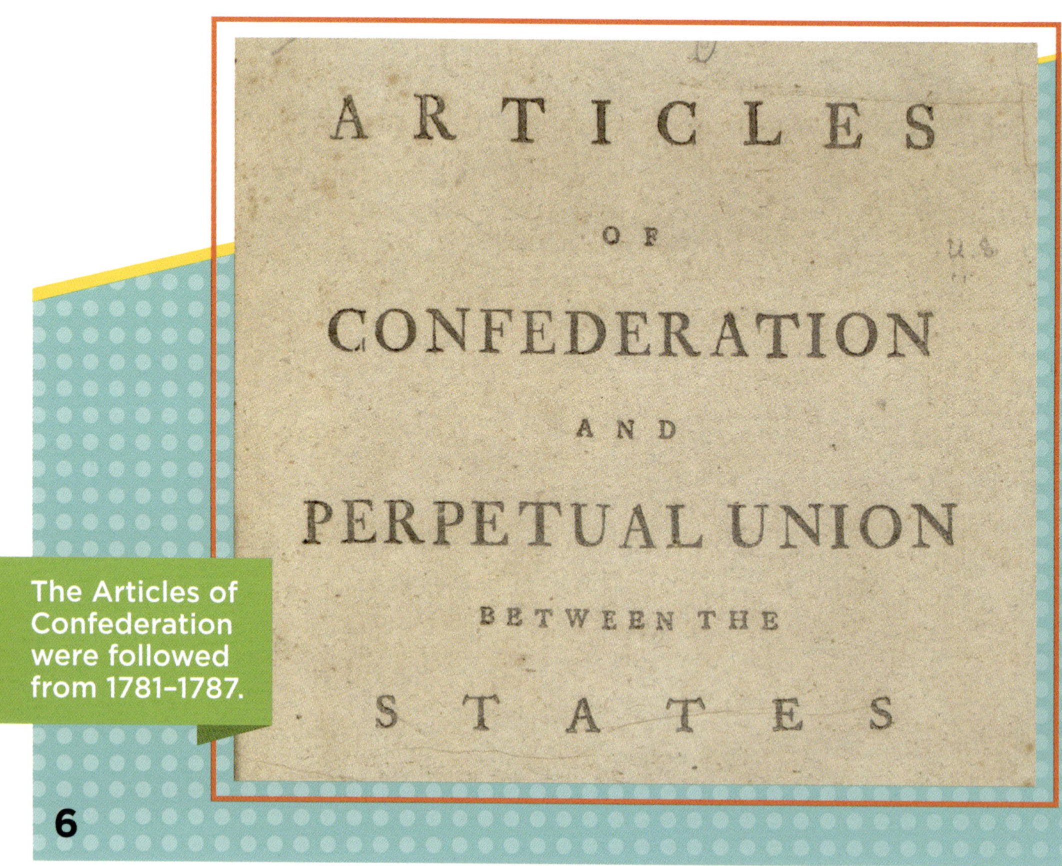
ARTICLES

OF

CONFEDERATION

AND

PERPETUAL UNION

BETWEEN THE

STATES

The Articles of Confederation were followed from 1781–1787.

Ask Questions!

Rulings by the Supreme Court impact all Americans. People worry about what the Supreme Court does to protect everyone's **human rights**. Read news articles about whose rights are protected and whose aren't. What do you think about this?

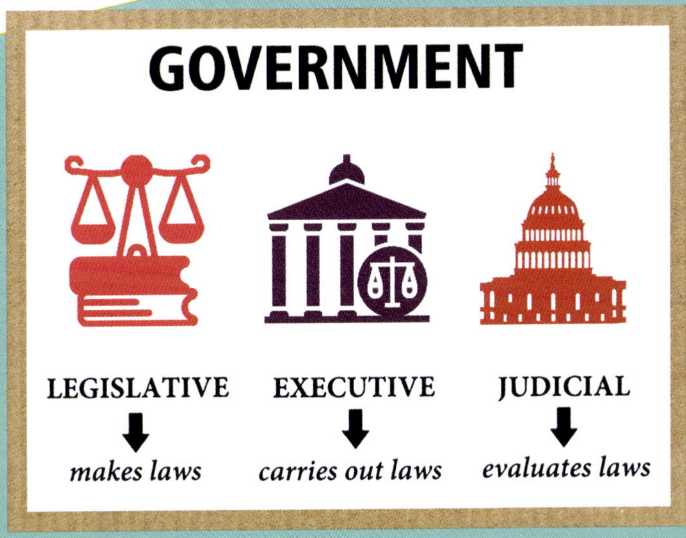

Realizing a court system would help **evaluate** and **interpret** laws, the country's founders created the Supreme Court. It's a necessary part of the government's system of **checks and balances**.

This system makes sure that none of the three government branches—executive, legislative, and judicial—have total power.

The Supreme Court has nine justices, or judges. The president **appoints** these justices. They are approved by Congress. It's important that justices are fair-minded. Their rulings affect everyone.

Nine justices serve on the United States Supreme Court.

Once a person becomes a Supreme Court justice, they serve for life. This is different from others in office. For instance, the president can only serve up to 8 years. Senators must be re-elected every 6 years.

Think!

Supreme Court justices can keep their jobs for their whole lives. Because of this, they have a big impact on U.S. history. Why do you think it's important that justices are fair-minded?

SUPREME COURT DUTIES

The Supreme Court's main job is to make sure laws follow the Constitution. The justices try to understand how laws affect different people in the United States.

The Supreme Court receives thousands of court cases each year. But the justices only take on a case when at least four of

CASES
UNADJUDICATED
1880 — 1882
CASES
UNADJUDICATED
1883 —
1885
IMPORTANT
CASE

No cameras are allowed in during arguments. Sketch artists like Art Lien draw what happens.

them agree to hear it. They read documents from lawyers and hear their arguments. The justices then discuss the case with one another.

After discussing, the justices vote. Many times, the nine justices don't agree on the final decision. But whichever side has five or more votes wins.

When the Supreme Court makes a decision, it's called a **ruling**. Once a ruling is made, it provides legal guidance for courts and legislators.

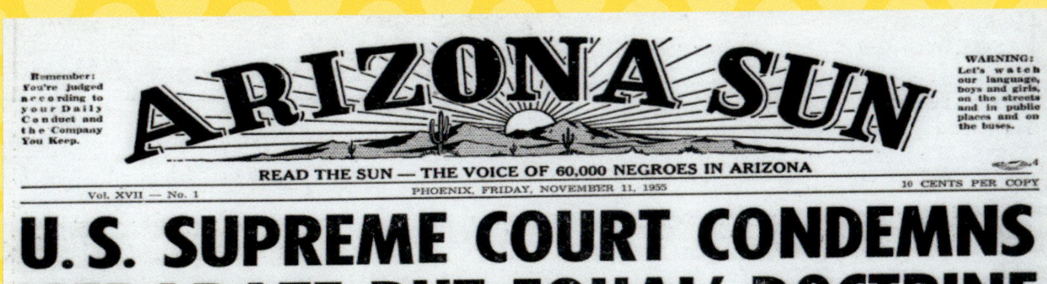

Remember: You're judged according to your Daily Conduct and the Company You Keep.

ARIZONA SUN

WARNING: Let's watch our language, boys and girls, on the streets and in public places and on the buses.

READ THE SUN — THE VOICE OF 60,000 NEGROES IN ARIZONA

Vol. XVII — No. 1 PHOENIX, FRIDAY, NOVEMBER 11, 1955 10 CENTS PER COPY

U. S. SUPREME COURT CONDEMNS 'SEPARATE BUT EQUAL' DOCTRINE

'Arizona On Parade' To Publicize State Across The Nation

SEGREGATION OF RACES IN PUBLIC PARKS PLAYGROUNDS AND GOLF COURSES UNCONSTITUTIONAL

WASHINGTON, — The supreme court last Monday struck down racial segregation in public parks,

The supreme court's order said: "The judgments both of the court of appeals and the district court

Justice Ketanji Brown Jackson is sworn in as the first Black female justice in the court's history. She replaced Justice Breyer when he retired.

When a ruling is made, the justices who supported the decision write a **majority opinion**. The majority opinion explains why the ruling was made. The justices who disagreed with the ruling write a **dissenting opinion**. It explains why they disagree with the ruling.

THE SUPREME COURT AFFECTS KIDS

When people talk about the government, it may feel like it's just about adults. But that's not true. Government impacts kids too. Sometimes the Supreme Court hears cases involving kids.

In the 1960s, the Supreme Court protected students' freedom of speech. During one case, it ruled that students do not shed their rights at the schoolhouse gate. This means that students like you have rights including free speech.

Ask Questions!

Many court cases are about freedom of speech. Why is it important to have free speech? What do you think would happen if we didn't have freedom of speech in the United States?

Look!

In 1954, the Supreme Court ruled that racial segregation was unfair in a case called *Brown v. Board of Education*. Schools desegregated. Students of all races were able to attend school with each other. Why is this a good thing? Why should we protect this ruling?

ACTIVITY

Dig deeper! Supreme Court justices can't let their personal opinions affect their decisions on a case. They must look at each case through the lens of right and wrong. They must decide if a case follows or goes against the U.S. Constitution. Research a **landmark case**. What are your thoughts on the case? Can you separate your opinions on the case from relevant facts?

GLOSSARY

appoints (uh-POYNTS) puts in place

checks and balances (CHEKS AND BAH-luhn-sez) system of government that makes sure no branch has too much power

desegregated (dee-SEH-grih-gay-tuhd) stopping the segregation of people

dissenting opinion (dis-SEN-ting uh-PIN-yuhn) explanation of why justices disagree with a ruling

evaluate (i-VAL-yoo-wayt) to judge

human rights (HYOO-muhn RYTES) powers and freedoms that all people should have

interpret (in-TUHR-pruht) to explain so others understand

landmark case (LAND-mark KAYS) Supreme Court case that has had a lasting effect on the law and future cases

majority opinion (muh-JOR-uh-tee uh-PIN-yuhn) explanation of the supreme court ruling

ruling (ROO-ling) final decision in a supreme court case

segregation (seh-gruh-GAY-shuhn) act of separating one group of people from another based on things such as race, gender, or religion

FIND OUT MORE

Books

Baxter, Roberta. *The Creation of the U.S. Constitution.* Ann Arbor, MI: Cherry Lake Publishing, 2014.

Cheney, Lynne. *We the People.* New York, NY: Simon & Schuster, 2012.

Knutson, Julie. *Born in 1954: Oprah Winfrey and Sonia Sotomayor.* Ann Arbor, MI: Cherry Lake Publishing, 2014.

Levy, Debbie. *Becoming RBG: Ruth Bader Ginsburg's Journey to Justice.* New York, NY: Simon & Schuster Books for Young Readers, 2019.

Sotomayor, Sonia. *Turning Pages.* New York, NY: Penguin Young Readers Group, 2018.

Websites

Activities for Students & Families—Supreme Court of the United States

https://supremecourt.gov/visiting/activities.aspx

Ben's Guide to the U.S. Government

https://bensguide.gpo.gov

Let Ben Franklin guide you through the whos and whats of our government.

iCivics

https://icivics.org

Find out how you can be an informed and involved citizen.

INDEX

ABOUT THE AUTHOR

Kevin Winn is a children's book writer and researcher. He focuses on issues of racial justice and educational equity in his work. In 2020, Kevin earned his doctorate in Educational Policy and Evaluation from Arizona State University.